# Minding My Business

## How I Turned Grime into My Grind

By

Sharon Green

Copyright © 2022 by Sharon Green

All rights reserved. No part of this book may be used or reproduced by any means, graphic, electronic, or mechanical, including photocopying, recording, taping, or by any information storage retrieval system, without the written permission of the publisher except in the case of brief quotations embodied in critical articles and reviews.

**Published By: Janay Roberson**
**Awaken U Publishing**
**www.janayroberson.com**

**ISBN:** 979-8-9870624-0-1
Printed in the United States of America

# Table of Contents

**Introduction** ............................................................................. 5

**Chapter 1:** The Big Picture Questions ............................................ 15

**Chapter 2:** How Much Will It Cost? .............................................. 18

**Chapter 3:** Time to Network ....................................................... 22

**Chapter 4:** Let's Get Down to Business ......................................... 25

**Chapter 5:** The Power of Social Media .......................................... 40

**Closing Thoughts: Launch Day** .................................................... 50

*In Loving Memory of*
**Aunt Freda Williams**

**Dedicated to Orlando, Jarian, Jordan and Calix.**

*You are my inspiration for all that I do.*

# Introduction

Everyone hates dirt—not just you, certainly not just me, but everyone. We can't stand to see it on our floors, carpets, back porches, sheets, bathroom tiles, or anywhere.

When I was working a full-time job, nothing made me as mad as coming home to a dirty house. If you grew up wondering why your mama yelled so loud when you tramped dirt into the house on your shoes after school, now, as an adult, you know why. Because she was dog tired from working all day and had to clean up after your sorry butt.

Dirt and its universal hatred inspired my revelation. I sat at my desk one day on my lunch break thinking I wasn't really using my full potential. There was more to life than what I was currently doing, and I knew there was something more out there for me, even if I couldn't see it clearly at the moment.

I had just graduated, earning my second degree. I had a major in business management and a minor in finance, and I had just battled my way through a bunch of business classes that taught me one inescapable truth: I was destined to be a leader. The problem was I couldn't put my finger on what I was actually passionate about. I could see the destination, but that first step in the journey was still eluding me. I knew I wanted something

I could call my own and leave as a legacy to my kids, but the identity of this mysterious endeavor was elusive.

More than anything, I knew I wasn't meant to simply work for someone else for the rest of my life. I didn't want to continue just being another spoke in the big wheel of a company, getting handed assignments and having my self-worth dictated by how much of a Christmas bonus I got at the end of each year. I needed to go beyond that, to the point where I was calling the shots, making the big-picture decisions, and dictating my destiny at the head of my own company.

Entrepreneurship has always been part of my life; to be honest, you could say it exists in my DNA. My grandparents and so many people in our family inspired me by running their own businesses. My grandmother owned her own beauty salon for more than thirty years. Talk about a dream business for a young girl growing up! Women would come in and trade gossip while they had their skin, hair, and nails serviced.

My grandfather owned his own construction company, allowing him to bid for jobs directly, rather than having to get a cut of every dollar taken out of his pocket by a foreman. In time, my father owned a car wash, and my uncles owned a car repair shop. My kin were hustling in their own time and space, working hard to be their own bosses and control their own fates in business.

From a young age, I learned the ins and outs of entrepreneurship, especially how much work it took, how detail-oriented you had to be, and how passionate you had to be about that business to ensure you never, ever lost the feeling of excitement and drive to succeed. If you lose that, it stops being your love and starts being just work.

On Saturdays, my grandmother would come for me and take me with her to the shop to get her client book. I'd be in charge of tallying up all of her income for the week and paying out the expenses. She was sort of tricking me into doing business math, but I didn't even care. I loved seeing how much her weekly profit was and sharing it with her when the news was good. I never thought about going into business for myself at that point. I had big dreams of being a lawyer as a kid. When I got to high school, I flirted with the idea of joining the military, but something about adding up those figures for my grandmother stayed with me, and I wound up going to college to major in accounting. I wasn't passionate about it, per se, but I knew it was a practical major that would get me a good job making good money, and I would never be hurt for work.

That was a very practical frame of mind for someone so young, but once I got out into the real world, I realized swiftly that accounting was not my passion. It was too boring, and I had way too big of a personality to sit quietly on a computer in the back room adding up numbers all day.

I dumped accounting and took a job in finance as an assistant manager, and my skill set got me moving more swiftly. Six months into my new job, they transferred me to Chattanooga,

Tennessee to become a branch manager, and I hadn't even turned 21 yet! I kept moving up the corporate ladder, becoming a regional supervisor with eight stores and more than 50 employees calling me boss.

I made history as the youngest supervisor in company history, and, while I was proud of that accomplishment, it still wasn't really scratching me where I truly itched. I decided to try another angle in the same company and wound up as an internal auditor. It was a big hit for me, and I thought it was my dream job. I was traveling, meeting new people, and solving problems—three things I really enjoyed doing. That passion lasted for about three years until I got a new job—arguably the best job on the planet—becoming a mom to my beautiful baby boy.

Suddenly, all the traveling as an auditor was negative, instead of positive because I was always headed off on a plane, missing precious moments with my son that would never, ever come back. I couldn't keep doing that to him or myself. So that's why I sat at my desk during lunch that day thinking there had to be something more for me, where I could utilize all my skills and still have lots of time for my family.

That's when I had my a-ha moment. That tickle at the base of my brain stem made me realize that instead of getting told where to go and what to do, I could go into business for myself and start running the show the way I had always wanted to.

The only thing holding me back at that point was what to sell and how to get going on my grind.

I didn't dream about being a business owner. Initially, I liked my job. I loved my family life. I liked my free time, and I was content. Then I wasn't. I had done some cleaning when I was younger for my Aunt Freda for extra cash but had never thought much more about it. Then one day, a friend of mine, Amanda Mayo, to whom I owe so much, contacted me and asked if I knew anyone who knew how to do a dorm flip—basically getting college dorm rooms ready for a new crop of students to move in when the new semester starts on campus.

The only thing she needed was to have the dorms cleaned. I jokingly said I was the person she was looking for because I had experience, and I was looking for a way to make some money to take a vacation. To my mild surprise, Amanda said that would be great, and the very next day, I had a meeting with the Chief Financial Officer of her company to talk about the job. I felt it would be a shot in the dark, but I went into that meeting as if I was the only candidate. I put all of my passion and enthusiasm into my presentation.

Something in my presentation struck a huge chord with the CFO, and she said not only did she want to give me that job, but she also wanted me to clean all assets of her property management company. In twenty-four hours, I went from making a humorous comment about doing some extra work to having a massive business opportunity literally dropped into my lap.

Since I've always been a people person, I knew I could ask for help and that people would respond. The first call I made was to my insurance agent, Stephanie Sinkfield, who not only gave me a quote about insurance for a business but also gave me a great pep talk on going into business for myself. She became one of three mentors—all women—who were guiding lights for me throughout the next few years.

Once I had those creative juices flowing, I wasn't going to stop until I was open for business. I called my husband that same day and told him I thought I had an idea for a business. He was incredibly supportive and 100 percent all in with me, ready to do what was necessary to make this new dream a reality. For the next twenty-four hours, I used GoDaddy.com to set up my website, Vistaprint to order my business cards, and set up social media accounts for my business so I could connect to customers in whatever manner they chose to do business. My husband, who has a degree in marketing, was an incredible resource for ideas and step-by-step guidance. I couldn't have done any of this without his support!

The next morning, my Facebook business page went live, and incredibly, I made my first customer outside of the property management company. Just like that! Then came the high-wire act part of the endeavor. I went to Wal-Mart with two friends and completely maxed out my Wal-Mart credit card with cleaning supplies and everything else I thought I would need for my business.

It was a gamble that paid off big time. From the first client cleaning the dorms, I found another property management company that was also looking for a cleaning service. Six months into the start of my business in 2018, we had grossed $76,000. That's when I realized this was becoming much more than a side hustle and, with the right energy and focus, it could turn into my main source of income.

As I went along the way, I had hoped to network with other owners of cleaning businesses to pick their brains. I wanted to see how they went about certain things, and how they overcame certain challenges, but I was in for a rude awakening. Not one cleaning business owner that I contacted had the slightest interest in talking to me! In hindsight, I think they were all fearful of the competition and having me use their best practices against them, but it always struck me as the wrong way to do things. In fact, it motivated me to write this book because I believe that shared knowledge is the best way forward for everyone to be successful. My mentors, including the aforementioned Stephanie Sinkfield, Carmen Davis, and Melinda Bone, did such an amazing job inspiring me to succeed that the best way to thank them is to pay it forward to other entrepreneurs.

In the second year, we hit $243,000. Keep in mind that was with no formal training on my part in this industry besides

Saturday morning cleanings at home growing up. But I busted my butt every night on the Internet, researching what to do and how to do it and making those critical decisions with my support team as my sounding board and rock throughout the process. I spent hours researching prices, chemicals, and equipment so that every single decision I made would maximize usage and minimize cost. I joined janitorial groups to get tips and tricks you would not get in everyday life.

I also made a lot of mistakes. I hired the wrong people sometimes. I wasn't prepared for how quickly everything took off. In one year, I went from two employees to over 20, and I was approached by different investors who wanted to either turn my business into a franchise or buy it outright!

Things were sailing along when 2020 arrived, and like every other businessperson out there, suddenly I found myself having to contend with the real possibility of the shutdown of my burgeoning business. I had to pause for a while because all my commercial clients canceled, but I was not going to let my dream just fall apart.

We lost one market, so we found the next one—COVID cleaning. I took some training and got educated on what it meant to clean something to the point of acceptability in the era of COVID-19 and we made that into our new offering. From tragedy rose opportunity, not only because of the pandemic but also from a tornado that hit the city and did significant damage, requiring a lot of refurbishments of home and apartment buildings, which saw property management companies calling upon us to assist. By the end of Year 3, we were grossing at close to half a million dollars with three shifts of cleaners working around the clock.

It hasn't all been butterflies and rainbows. There have been times I've had to dip into my personal finances to pay my employees their wages when one of our clients didn't pay on time. That's a lot of stress on anyone, but my biggest point of pride in running this business is that I am giving people a safe, fair, solid place to work and earn a living. We hire people who sometimes have small infractions on their background checks but are good people who just need someone to give them a chance. Just because they don't have a degree doesn't mean they can't be great team leaders or team managers. I have taught them skills to give them the chance to do more with their lives and be a bigger part of the company.

That team spirit has paid off with awards, including the Chattanooga Times Free Press Newspaper Best of the Best Award. We won a similar award from the local Channel 3 News station. We were the first winner of the BEC Best Cleaning Company Award and have been featured on the front page of the business section of the local newspaper. We pay that forward by reinvesting in the community. My company sponsors baseball, basketball, and cheerleading teams in the area. I personally mentor several rising entrepreneurs, many in the same industry as mine. I believe fervently in the idea that to whom much is given, much is expected.

Maybe you're like me. You have realized working for someone else just isn't your dream. Maybe you've decided to take another route. Perhaps you knew from the beginning you wanted to be the boss, but you've never had the courage to admit it to yourself or anyone else. Well, guess what? Now's the time to take that leap of faith, and I'm here to show you how to do it. Now's the time to stop dreaming and start doing. This is your Business 101 Guide where you'll quickly learn how to launch your own company and start turning all those dreams into a reality.

# 1

## The Big Picture Questions

### What will your business look like?

Before you tell your boss to take this job and shove it, you have a lot of planning to do. You have to know what your business will look like and how you will get it started. Most importantly, you must spell out and understand what your business will be, what problem it solves, and who your customers will be. You might have the greatest idea in the world for a product or service, but truth be told, unless other people, and I mean many other people agree with you, your business is never going to get off the ground.

Your business must solve a problem people cannot solve on their own or do not want to do on their own because it's too expensive, time-consuming, or they just don't like it. There's a business I know called Poo Patrol that travels around the suburbs every week picking up dog poop from everyone's backyards. They charge based on the number of pets using your yard as a toilet every week. Now, people have had the simple tools and ability to clean up dog poop for centuries, but many people don't have the time to clean up dog poop or actually want to do it because, well, it's poop! Poo Patrol has found its niche and its customer base, and does great business with a solid profit margin as a result.

Your business does not have to be an original idea. You do not have to reinvent the wheel. My cleaning service was not the first one in the city, much less the first one ever. So what I had to do was figure out how I would differentiate my business from the competition, and that's something you will have to do as well. Is your business better? How? Do you offer better prices, lots of discounts, or better customer service? Do you provide services at unique hours or is your staff specially trained?

As you plan your business, you must figure out what separates you from everyone else. That's how you will market and sell yourself in the long run.

## How hands-on will you be?

In other words, will you be on the ground floor serving clients or in the comfortable chair running the show from the top down? Neither of these is the wrong answer. It has a lot more to do with who you are and what you envision for yourself. If you're a wedding cake designer, you will be pretty hands-on because your skill is selling the business. You might hire an assistant or a driver somewhere along the way, but the creative talent you bring to the table is what people will plunk down their money for.

If you are running a staffing agency for temporary workers, you might start by being very hands-on and gradually move into a role where you deal mainly with making the big-picture decisions. The layers of people underneath you handle the day-to-day activities like finding candidates, vetting them, staying in touch with employers, listing positions, and so on.

## Are you planning on working another job while you build your business?

This is often the toughest one to answer because, for most people, it is really difficult to commit 100 percent of their time to grow a new business. The main reason is they don't have enough money to invest in a new business while also paying the bills. Therefore, they think they have no choice but to keep on working that 9-to-5 grind and let the new business be a side hustle. That's fine if you aren't expecting your new business to be your full-time gig. However, if you don't give your new endeavor 100 percent of your attention, it will take a long time to develop it as you wish. Moreover, you'll likely miss out on many opportunities or someone may beat you to the punch with whatever your product/service is because you were too busy still punching the clock, instead of living your dream.

# 2

## How Much Will It Cost?

It should not come as any great surprise that while fear is the #1 reason most people don't start their own businesses; money is a strong #2. Most of us are living some version of paycheck to paycheck as we battle our ways through life. We try to be good and build that savings account and emergency fund, but it's a struggle.

Bad things seem to happen at the worst times. We get in a car wreck. Someone gets sick. COVID-19 happens. Someone gets laid off. We fear doing almost anything with our money besides paying our bills and putting it in the bank. It's a huge leap of faith to put your money into something else, especially something that has a chance of failing. That's a sobering fact we should take a closer look at before we dive deeper into the financial matters of a new business.

According to the US Bureau of Labor Statistics, 20 percent of new businesses will fail during the first two years they are open. That number rises to 45 percent in the first five years and 65 percent in the first 10 years. Only 1 in 4 businesses will make it to at least its 15th anniversary. Those are some daunting statistics, to say the least!

So let's talk about the best ways to start a business to avoid disaster and going broke in the process.

The first piece of advice I have for you is to get out of as much debt as possible before you start your business. That's not just good business sense; that's good life sense. All your creditors want you to be in debt for a long time because they're making money hand over foot off you, thanks to whatever interest rate you agreed to. If you have money left over when you pay your bills each month, and you also owe a lot in debt, don't worry about that business right now. Put it off for six months, a year, or even two, and use those extra dollars to knock down the principal on your debt. You will save yourself considerable long-term damage by doing so.

Depending on what sort of business you're going to start, your initial investment can vary greatly. The United States Small Business Administration (SBA) has done research that says most home-based businesses need between $2,000-$5,000 to start. They should also have about six months' worth of fixed costs on hand to ensure that they can stay afloat if the sales don't come streaming through the door as projected.

Your fixed costs include everything you need to keep that business going. If you will be running a traditional store, your fixed costs will be high because of the price of renting a space. If you set up a website, you will incur a cost for the domain name and maybe the website creation. If you're making products in your home, the fixed costs will include your supplies/ingredients, shipping costs, and potentially paying a helper or assistant. All of these things can weigh you down if you're not prepared. Therefore, writing a business plan first and foremost is essential. It will help you understand the entire scope of what you're trying to create.

You must also calculate how much you're going to be paying yourself as the employee of your new business. Take away the costs from the revenue to get your profits. If your sales aren't good and you only have $100 to show after each month, how will you keep paying your bills? You must find the balance between cutting costs and selling enough of your product/service to live on, and then some. Otherwise, what's the point?

As you move toward opening your business, you must secure a business bank account. One of the worst mistakes people make is using their personal checking account to double as their business account. This is a terrible mistake because none of us are good enough at numbers to keep our business transactions separate from our personal day-to-day transactions. Don't be impersonal and just sign up for a business account online, either. Go into your local branch;

meet a representative, and explain your plans and what you want to accomplish.

Most banks give extra perks for business accounts because, when you use them, you're investing money back into the local economy, which is always good for banks. If they can't give you the kind of account terms you want, shop around. There are banks all over the place that can meet your needs and give you a friendly face and sounding board as well.

Take the time to find a good bank that's the right fit for you. Remember, now you are a business owner, banks should pursue you as someone who can be a great asset to them. They should pursue you the way you pursue customers for your own business. If a bank seems less than enthusiastic about you opening a business account, that's your cue to walk out the door or hang up the phone. Banks that understand how important small businesses are in their communities will give you all kinds of perks, everything from free bill payments to no minimum balance requirements to unlimited monthly transactions to waiving fees on foreign transactions. They will offer you overdraft protection for times when your money in might be lagging behind your money out.

# 3

## Time to Network

Being an entrepreneur doesn't mean you have to build your business all by yourself. One of the best parts about the world of digital technology is that it's easy to find like-minded people who are also opening their own businesses or are further along the track than you are who are willing to help out. You don't even have to get out of your chair. There are lots of options online that you can use to bounce ideas off other business owners, get advice, or look for partnerships. Some of the more well-rounded places you can visit online to join an entrepreneurship community are:

Alignable: This is a referral network for small businesses where you can connect, ask for advice, and get referrals. It's free to join.

LinkedIn: Another site that is free to join and is great for networking. You can easily reach out and connect to other businesspeople and let them know you are searching for advice or a mentor. You might even find someone who wants to invest in your business.

The Fastlane Entrepreneur Forum: More than 60,000 entrepreneurs are on this site with a really busy forum that can really let you cover a lot of ground with a lot of minds.

Startups.com: It's right there in the name! Company founders and others join discussions, and the site runners vet you before you can post, meaning spamming isn't allowed.

If you prefer face-to-face communication, you can find lots of great people to connect with directly as well. Every city has local groups that meet to talk business, and it's as simple as doing a Google search or examining Facebook to find them. There are also groups known as accelerators where you can apply to be a part of their cause and get timely tips, possible financial support, and go through an intensive program that is designed to get your business off and running more quickly. These usually require applications and interviews for you to get approval, so don't just drop a note in the mail and think you're good to go. Accelerators only want the best, brightest, and most unique participants, so make sure you have an interesting story to share when you're up!

The Chamber of Commerce is another great resource when you're starting. Join one in your area. This is a group of businesses in a specific region that work together to bring awareness to their endeavors. They get together to contribute to charitable causes, have big events about once a month where you can go to hear a great speaker, have a free lunch, and do some top-quality networking. You can hand out business cards, give out free samples, and really meet people who can get your business noticed. I can't recommend contacting the Chamber of Commerce in your area enough!

# 4

# Let's Get Down to Business

We've gone through a lot of philosophical and psychological stuff here, the steps that get you to the starting line, but at this point, you need to make some big-time decisions that are going to affect the way your business appeals to people, how it is run, what it looks like to the IRS and other governing bodies, and so forth.

## Get a Business Name

Let's start with the simplest thing, which often can be the toughest to decide on: your company name.

You need one if you want to brand yourself and let people know you. You can't just be "John Smith does web design" or "Allison Davis makes cakes." You need a name that is easy to remember and tells what you do very clearly. If someone sees your business name on a sign, a business card, or a social media post and can't tell what kind of business it is in the first 2-3 seconds, you're sunk, and they're going to keep moving on to look somewhere else. A lot of people try to get too cute with their business names, with a play on words or a pop culture reference. Sometimes that works, and sometimes it doesn't. It really depends on the industry. A bakery can call its business "Cake It Easy" and people will probably still understand what it's about, but if you're running a business that replaces carpets, cleans chimneys, or repairs cars, you don't want people thinking you are silly and goofy with a funny business name.

When you think of a name, you must also make sure no one else has the same business name. This doesn't apply to the entire country, but make sure you're not invading someone else's space by picking a similar name. If you visit Northwestregisteredagent. com, it can help you go state by state and make sure you aren't infringing on anyone else's registered business name. Don't even think about trying to make your name close to a name brand in hopes of playing off their name recognition for yourself. Don't start a hamburger kitchen called Mack Donald's. Their lawyers are everywhere, and they will hunt you down and sue you for your last dime.

## Apply for DBE

Before you start spending money left and right, it is a smart idea to look into the Disadvantaged Business Enterprise Program (DBE). This is a government-sponsored endeavor to help minorities and women level the playing field when it comes to starting and operating a small business. You have to apply to the program, but it is well worth it if you do indeed qualify. Your business has to be at least 51 percent owned and operated by one or more US citizens or legal residents who are classified as socially or economically disadvantaged according to certain criteria, including being a racial minority or a woman. It also includes people who have a net worth of less than $1.32 million, have three years of gross receipts for an existing business that are less than $28.48 million combined, or have a person in one of those aforementioned disadvantaged groups who is either the owner, holds the highest position, handles the firm's day-to-day business, or has technical expertise in the firm's primary business activities.

Getting approved for a DBE status will help draw attention to your business, especially if you deal with contracts from any level of the government. The idea is to get more competition out there for government contracts that don't discriminate against a business because it's owned by a racial minority, a woman, or someone who has not been in business for very long.

You might not initially think about contracts with the government when you start your business, but the government on every level is one of the largest employers in every city and state in the country. The government at the local, county, state, and federal levels always needs good services and products at great prices for cleaning office buildings, servicing vehicles, providing catering services, office supplies, entertainment for department events, and so forth. Therefore, if you have a product or service you can provide, you are a great candidate for a government contract.

If you qualify for the DBE, all you need to do is get informed and fill out an application to be licensed. That gives you a chance to get lots of extra work contracts. It's always great to do research for opportunities like this, particularly if you are a minority or woman business owner. There are lots of efforts underway to try and rebalance and make small businesses more diverse, so if you have the opportunity to get a loan, a grant, or a chance for better opportunities to gain customers in your business, by all means, do it!

## Get a Business License

Depending on what kind of business you plan on running, you'll need a business license. This is true, especially if you are operating a brick-and-mortar location (a physical store), hiring employees, offering health insurance, or anything like that. The more complex your business is, the more licenses you will need. The Small Business Administration offers the best resources for you to understand what you need in your area and industry.

## Determine Your Business Structure

You also need to determine the structure of your business. You can have a very basic one that doesn't even need to be registered, or register as a corporation, which has lots of advantages as well.

The simplest type of structure is the sole proprietorship, which means it's your business and you have total control. You don't have to register as any sort of business. It also means that your assets and liabilities are the same as that of your business. That can be risky if your business is sued because the those suing can come after your personal money and belongings if they win.

A partnership means you have one or more other people who also own at least part of the business. The most common kinds are Limited Partnerships (LPs) and limited liability partnerships (LLPs). LPs typically mean that one general partner has unlimited liability, and the rest have liability based on how much of the company they own. For example, if someone owns 25 percent of the company, he would only be responsible for 25 percent of a fine or a lawsuit settlement. An LLP gives limited liability to every owner, meaning he is not responsible for the actions of someone else that costs the company money.

A very popular structure for people in business on their own is to form a Limited Liability Company (LLC). This creates a separate entity just for your business that is not tied to you in any way. Someone who ate the wedding cake you made and had an allergic reaction may try to sue you, but the person can only come after the assets that belong to the company, not your personal property.

## Apply for an EIN

Your next step is to apply for an Employer Identification Number (EIN) from the IRS. Dealing with the IRS can be a little worrisome for most people, but you must realize if you want to do business the right way, they are just one more organization you need to partner with. Your EIN is a unique number that identifies you as a business owner and lets you pay your taxes easily. If someone tries to sell you an EIN number or says you have to pay to get one, it's a scam. You can apply for free on the IRS website.

## Register Your Business Name

You're not quite done yet, as you also need to register your business name with the Secretary of State of the state that you live in. This isn't mandatory in all states, but it helps solidify the fact that you are a business owner in the case of disputes or if someone tries to copycat your business. This is an essential step if you are creating unique products or trademarking your business or your brand. Protect yourself legally. Otherwise, people will try to take advantage and steal from you if you have a great business idea or name.

## Consider Business Insurance

Depending on the type of business you start, business insurance could be a huge issue or a non-issue. If you're a freelance writer sitting at a computer all day, you will not need business insurance, other than if your computer breaks down. However, if you have a physical location, you should definitely get business insurance for protection against fire, floods, theft, vandalism, and other risks. Any equipment or vehicles you use should also be insured so you don't have to pay the full cost to replace or repair them.

You should also consider getting insurance in the event an employee gets hurt on the job and can no longer work. This is called workman's compensation and is essential if you want to be viewed as a legitimate business. In many states, it's illegal to hire employees without this type of coverage. That sort of insurance should also extend to your customers. If someone slips and falls on melted ice on the floor of your restaurant, and you are sued, insurance protects you against such things.

## Have Social Media Presence

Before you get going on your first day of business, you must absolutely have a presence on social media and a fully functional website for promotion. You should be visible on as many social media sites as makes sense, particularly Facebook and Instagram as they are very visual and it is easy to get a following by posting photos of products and services. You can easily interact with customers and potential customers, as well, and make sales on your phone or online, instead of having to pound the pavement.

Incredibly, only about <u>71 percent of businesses have websites.</u> That is a huge mistake on the part of the ones who don't. How many times have you seen a sign or heard about a business and punched it into Google for a closer look? If the search results come up empty, most of us think the business isn't real or invested enough in its customers to have a website, and that's a big strike three.

If you don't have a website at this point, get out a permanent marker and the biggest sticky note you can find and write in all caps, "GET A WEBSITE IMMEDIATELY!"

Now that you've reminded yourself, let's assume you have a website up and running, or you've at least registered for a free bit of space on the Internet through a site like WordPress. It's important to have a lot of relevant information on your website, but do you know what's even more crucial to your search for great leads? A visually appealing website will encourage visitors to spend more time browsing your site. That way, they will learn more about you and want to do business with you.

Let's be superficial for a moment here. If you're single and at a bar or a party, probably the first thing you notice about someone of the opposite sex is what he looks like. If he is attractive, interesting looking, or has a great smile or something about him that is unique and appealing to you, the chances that you'll buy him a drink or go up and talk to him absolutely skyrockets at that moment. The same is true of a website! If you visit a website full of drab colors, boring text, outdated photos, and an overall lack of pizazz, there is a very small chance you will give that company your business. Is it fair? Who cares? It's a reality your website must embody your sense of professionalism, style, and appeal to get leads.

How fast do people judge if they want to continue browsing a website? Scary fast. According to industry data, they know within five one-hundredths of a second. In the time it takes you to count to one, a person has already determined if your website is worth their time and has either moved in or moved on.

According to Research Gate, it's not just that first burst either: 94 percent of first impressions of websites are based on how they look.[1] The worst thing you can do with your website is to take the cheap route, which means only taking the free option from a hosting site. The only thing as bad as no website is having a boring one. You are indirectly telling your potential leads you're boring and blasé and don't understand how valuable the Internet is to business.

Most people treat a website the way they used to treat newspapers—their eyes will stay "above the fold." For a newspaper, that means the news stories at the top of the page will get read the most. For a website, it means the first thing

---

[1] https://websitebuilder.org/blog/website-design-industry-statistics/

that appears will be seen the most and hold the most value. If visitors to your website have to scroll down to see more information, it's unlikely they will.

What many web designers have found is you may have big, bold headlines promising great services on your website, but most people are drawn more to photos, specifically photos of people in your design.2 Perhaps it's the humanity in all of us that we are drawn to other people's faces and body language as a barometer for how the page strikes us. A picture of a clean house might interest some people, but it's the way we feel about enjoying that clean house that is a real lynchpin in this process.

Whether you plan to hire someone to design your website; you will take it on yourself, or you will have a friend or family member help you out, here are a few tips that will go a long way toward helping you get a great-looking attractive site up and running.

## No Clutter

Don't design a cluttered or complex website. Have you ever been to a site with five or six different little sections and sliders that you can move around? It makes our skin crawl, quite honestly. The designer might have thought it was smart to put as much information as possible on one page to appeal to a

---

2 https://blog.marketing360.com/design-and-branding/how-to-use-human-faces-in-your-website-design-tips-examples-from-marketing-360/

wide range of audiences, but the opposite winds up happening. Visitors don't know where to look or what is most important, and they end up leaving the site for something easier to understand. Avoid that by using just one column of information all the way down the page. This makes it very easy to follow and leaves no doubts about the progress of the narrative.

## Let Others Speak for You

It's a lot better to let others speak for you than to speak for yourself. One of the hardest things for most businesspeople to do on their websites is to write about how great a job they do. It makes them feel as if they are bragging, and for many people that is a really tough thing to do. Some will hire a third-party content writer to concoct their web copy, but that can be ineffective since that person hasn't seen them in action. The obvious thing people miss in this space is that the very best form of advertising now, 50 years ago, and 500 years ago remains word of mouth.

When genuine, real people use your service and have great experiences, their words carry more weight than a billion billboards or a gazillion Google Ads. Reviews are a proven lead attractor because people inherently trust other people's real opinions, even if they are people they have never met or will ever meet a day in their lives. Research shows that 84 percent of people trust online reviews as much as they trust their friends.3 It makes sense. If people have profoundly good experiences using your service, they are typically the kind of people who are conscious of sharing that information with the community at large. Just as likely they will do so if they have an unsatisfactory experience.

You might be excited to have sterling reviews on Yelp, Facebook, or some other platform, but why would you want your leads to hunt and peck everywhere for those reviews when you can condense them all into one central location—your website? Find a way to display them beautifully and simply. Don't let people have to search for the great things others are saying about you.

## Be Visually Appealing in a Subtle Way

Rainbows and sparkles might work well to get kids to visit the ice cream parlor or the carnival rides, but adults have a more refined sense of what draws the eye to a website. Just like everyone suggests painting the inside of your house white before you sell it, your website should be largely white to keep the focus on the images and the most important words. Only use colors if you want to direct the viewer's attention to a very specific point on the page, for example, a button or video.

If you prefer, replace the all-white with an all-dark theme, where the whole screen is black and the text is white. It's the

---

3 https://www.adzooma.com/blog/why-we-trust-the-opinions-of-strangers-on-the-internet/

same principle and many people say they can read text better in this format.

## Don't Ask for Too Much Information

Avoid asking people for too much information by requesting it in a bunch of fields on your website. The more people have to spend time typing in information and giving away the farm when it comes to their name, phone number, email address, etc., the more likely they will feel you will turn around and sell their information to a bunch of spam artists.

Is there anything more annoying than searching Google for information, finding a great website, and then having it overwritten by a banner ad demanding your name and contact information before you can continue? It drives us nuts, and we should definitely learn from our experiences as customers how to behave better as business owners attracting leads.

Now, don't get rid of the fill-in fields completely because the more information you have from someone, the easier it is to get them started down the user journey to converting a sale. Find a way to balance the number of fields with the bare minimum of information needed. Be smart and realize most people have a Google account or a Facebook profile that already has all that information saved. If you give them the option to integrate one with the other, all they have to do is click a button to sign up for whatever registration or contact form you've provided. If you want to request more information, make sure you've got a really tasty carrot to dangle in front of their noses to make it a worthwhile exchange. It could be a coupon for a local freebie, a free consultation, or something else, but don't expect to earn a deeper level of contact information for free.

## Outline Your Website's Look

Outline what your website should look like and ensure every page has a singular purpose. Don't mix and match the information on different pages. Keep it simple on the front page and the contact page. When people keep seeing that "Contact Us!" bubbles appear; it annoys them. People are smart; they don't need constant reminders of how a website works.

## Keep Your Website Simple

Some people will come to your website frequently and treat it as a trusted resource. Others will stumble on it and take a single glance. Therefore, your site must be simple enough to get both types of visitors to take the next step of the customer journey where you can contact them. Your goal for any and all visitors is to become a trusted resource.

## Get Business Cards

Just because the whole world has gone digital, it doesn't mean the old ways of marketing are extinct. They still work. Business cards are dirt cheap to make these days. You can get 500 for a few dollars. Carry them around with you everywhere and always have them within reach when you meet someone new. That lets you shake their hand and give them a card at the same time. Having social media and a website is great, but that little piece of stiff paper is tangible. People will stick it in their pockets, purses, or wallets. Later, when they need your product or service they will contact you. Nothing is a bigger conversation killer than someone asking if you have a business card and you saying no.

Depending on your type of business, you can get creative with other types of marketing material. If you are active in your community, you can print T-shirts and give them away at a community event like a festival or have your logo put on drink koozies, Frisbees, or water bottles. You can advertise in local community newspapers or magazines or ask for a story to be done on your business; all they can do is say no!

## Advertise on Your Car

Pay for a company to stencil your company's name, logo (if you have one), and phone number or website on your car. Then you can drive everywhere and do your own marketing. People will stop you to ask for more information!

Opportunities abound everywhere, but you must think outside the box and realize the more you get your name out there, the more successful you will be.

# 5

## The Power of Social Media

We touched on social media in the last section and how important having an online presence is. While most people have at least one or two social media accounts to keep up with friends and family, watch the latest trends in their favorite pastimes, and so forth, a lot of entrepreneurs simply aren't aware of what a massive amount of business you can acquire from social media, without spending any real money on it. The real cost of acquiring customers by social media is often your time and creativity, so if you have both, you can make things pay off!

Social media, as a smaller component of the Internet itself, has become a great equalizer in business. You can run a company from your 10-square-foot home office and make it every bit as professional and well-respected as a massive corporation if you know how to harness the enormous powers of social media and digital technology. The real business owners who realize this are commanding legions of followers and are constantly getting their names recommended to others via every channel imaginable: text, email, word of mouth, Facebook, Twitter, Instagram, LinkedIn, Yelp, you name it.

The simple fact is that using social media allows you to duck under the "velvet rope" at the mythical club and straight into the personal confidence of people. Social media is a massive industry run largely by algorithms and bots, but the very heart of it is people connecting to other people in an informal way that garners trust, and lets you talk plainly about your ambitions, hopes, and dreams. It should be the alpha and omega of every single person in every single industry trying to sell a product or service.

The amount of legwork that can be avoided in traditional marketing and sales by having a strong social media presence cannot be overstated. It should be no surprise that Facebook continues to see the most return on investment for marketers. About 40 percent of them said it was their No. 1 moneymaker in Hubspot's 2021 State of Marketing report. Instagram checks in at No. 2, followed by LinkedIn, YouTube, Twitter, and Snapchat a surprising sixth. It's smarter to pick several of these platforms than just one, largely because they are mostly owned by one another and people who have one social media account tend to have multiple accounts, meaning you can really play up brand recognition by approaching them via multiple channels.

Facebook is the classic example of a company that can "take a licking and keep on ticking." Despite multiple high-level scandals and creator Mark Zuckerberg often looking like a tone-deaf bazillionaire, the company has billions of users and other than Google and Amazon, is probably the most well-known company in the world, even as it rebrands itself Meta and starts a move toward creating the VR-based metaverse. What's actually a little shocking is how few small businesses in the US use Facebook for advertising. As of 2020, that number was 10 million, which seems high until you realize there are about 32 million small businesses in the United States, according to the Small Business Administration.

Ask yourself the easiest question in the world to answer: if there was a place where billions of people went every day, but only about one out of every three of your competitors was advertising there, wouldn't that be a good place for you to head?

You don't need a degree in marketing to run a Facebook profile for your real estate business. What you need to do is be authentic. Don't be a marketing troll when people accept your friend requests. Be a real person sharing your life with your circle of connections—the personal and professional stuff.

When you see friends for lunch, when you take a trip, when you have a spa day, when you celebrate a birthday or an anniversary, when you meet a new person who is going to become part of your professional circle, it should all be celebrated on Facebook.

That lets people who connect with you see you are genuine and not just lurking in the social media hub to try to get their money for your business. In the gaps of doing that, you need to share professional content that will let people see you as the guru of your business in your marketplace.

You don't have to do 10 posts a day, nothing over the top like that. However, post what's interesting to you and insightful about the industry you are in. You can take that content and convert it to a look that is suitable for your Instagram page or Twitter account. You can even record yourself talking about it and make it into a TikTok or a YouTube video. Most people go on Facebook for family and fun and to expand their knowledge base. If you can do all three, you will find some amazing leads who will feel as if they already know you before you first shake their hands. Use other social media platforms to follow popular trends, users, and series, and repost them to your Facebook page. Don't just post things at random or at 3 a.m. when you can't sleep, though. You want to maximize the number of reads, clicks, and likes you get by posting new things when you know people are most likely to be on Facebook. That's universally in the morning and early in the week. Basically, we're celebrating the fact that everyone gets to work around 9 a.m. and instantly starts checking social media feeds, instead of doing actual work! Lunchtime, between 11 a.m. and 1 p.m. is also a hotbed as people take their breaks and catch up on life outside of the office. If you're posting late at night or on the weekends, you're pretty much wasting your time. Even if people are checking their alerts at these intervals, it's usually while they're doing something more engaging. Your posts might get a glance, but they will be forgotten.

Don't forget about engagement, either! Check your mentions, responses, and reposts frequently. Always identify those who mentioned you, and mention them in kind. Call them by their first names, @ them in your reply so they get an alert as well. Follow up with a question or a comment of your own that will enhance the chance they will respond again or others will join the discussion. Presenting yourself as affable and approachable online delivers the idea that this is how you are in "real life" as well, It will inspire strangers to gravitate to you with their problems and questions.

If you think your feed is stagnant, a quick trick is to ask a question that people want to respond to and use it as a springboard to other posts and more relevant discussions. You'll get a bevy of answers—some serious, some hilarious. And you will be able to engage a lot of people in fun, introspective discussions that will get you more information about them and let them get to know you better. This information can be used to form deeper connections that can lead to real estate discussions if appropriate.

When your Facebook Messenger gives you an alert, get on it as fast as you can. Treat it as if your phone is ringing and it might be an important call on the other end.

Engaging with people as they are thinking about you and your posts is the surefire way to make them recognize you value relationships and are willing to help them in whatever way you can. Even if it's just an "I like your picture!" message, that is a classic breaking-the-ice technique people use before asking what they really want to know. They want to see if you are as genuine and approachable as you seem in your posts. When you share other people's posts, it is a natural ego booster for them. They will more likely return the favor and make a stronger connection with you. That kind of personal touch creates a great impression on lots of people.

Let's also consider some things you absolutely should not do when you're using your own Facebook page to market your business. Never drag political or controversial subjects into your business posts.

As polarized as the American political landscape has been over the past ten years or so, the last thing you want to do is alienate 50 percent of your potential leads by hammering one official or praising another. Keep your opinions limited to your family and friends, and do not post something online that you will regret ten minutes later. Facebook is not the place for you to be flying off the handle. Your posts should be considerate and compassionate.

If Facebook isn't your thing or if you want to get on several social media networks, stretch out to Instagram, YouTube, TikTok, and Twitter. You know your strengths best and you should know your market best as well. If you are young and your client base typically trends that way as well, focus on TikTok and Instagram as your bellwether cows.

## Twitter

Twitter is perhaps the most informal of all social media interactions because of the short limit on the number of characters you can produce. It's also one of the easiest ways to remind people about the actual human being who stands behind your brand and gives you the great option of talking publicly or privately with people. But don't mix up those two! More than anything, Twitter is a great way for you to stay educated and up to date about topics, news, and people who are important to your role in the industry. Following organizations that keep track of the industry trends and economic indicators can fill you to the brim with knowledge you can convert into great blogs, posts, videos, and simple conversations. While Twitter still limits the number of characters, the hot trend of Twitter threads lets you circumvent that and create a sort of email chain letter through social media. You can start with a tweet and keep building it longer and longer like a traditional storyteller. Your followers and contacts can add commentary, ask questions, and engage you directly as you move along.

As with every other form of presentation, your ability to work in videos, pictures, relevant links, and the always-popular animated GIF is a great way to attract attention and drive engagement.

## Instagram

Breaking news! Instagram isn't just for sharing pictures of what you ordered for dinner last night or taking "duck-lips" pictures with your friends. A good Instagram account can be as profitable for free as a strong Facebook profile. The problem most professionals have with IG is that they don't know how to post, how often to post, or who to appeal to.

Instagram Stories is a wonderful tool. You are crafting a narrative for people to follow along, rather than just producing a one-time, hit-or-miss post. A great way to get people interested in your IG post is to work a poll into it. People love to have their opinions solicited and love to see how they match up with the others in the poll. When you include one, not only will you be getting people engaged but more than likely they will return to check on the results over time to see how their choices are stacking up. All the bells and whistles you can attach to an Instagram story: tags, links, GIFS, questions, and locations, build the personality and intimacy of your post. They will cause more people to gravitate toward you as you connect with them on multiple levels.

Instagram reels are also on the cutting edge of the social media universe. They have a much better reach than a post combined with a video because they are the best of both worlds. Micro-content is a real thing. Imagine it being like a food sample at the ice cream parlor that gives you a hint of the flavor and convinces you to buy two scoops in the cone. A 10-second Instagram reel is the maximum length you should use to get people's interest without saddling them with a longer video. Hashtag it and pull their interests precisely where you want them to be.

## TikTok

TikTok's rapid growth is even more of a miracle when you think how many dozens of social media newcomers there have been over the years who have vanished off the map almost as quickly as they appeared. TikTok has just about everything, and even if you are like us and initially thought it was just for kids, its non-stop evolution and ridiculous growth should have convinced you otherwise by now. TikTok is the definition of the phrase going viral, and people all over the globe are using it to showcase their expertise in a million different subjects.

TikTok is the home of smart content that goes to niche markets in a very short format. You don't need high production values. In fact, many people will like it more if it's just your talking head telling them hacks for getting the best home mortgage rate or how to stretch $100 into a week's worth of home-cooked meals. Make sure you add some bells and whistles to your video, but not to the point that they are distractions. There's an Internet full of free music that serves as a nice ambiance behind your words. Find something you like and use it repeatedly to make it your brand. If you have some sort of bonus information, add a little effect, a silly sound, or a sticker to let viewers know it's something extra just for them. Stand out!

## LinkedIn

You might feel you don't need LinkedIn unless you're looking to move back to the corporate sector, but LinkedIn has evolved in its own unique ways over the years. Many professionals seek professional services outside of hiring or looking for a job on LinkedIn. It's a great place to establish yourself as a subject-matter expert (SME) and a great place to network with other professionals who can make your business that much better. You can endorse people's skills, promote your own products—like this book, for instance—and branch out beyond your backyard into a larger network of interrelated professionals who are seeking to grow their own businesses in a similar fashion.

Your posts here are definitively professional, not personal, and you're always on the lookout for people willing to trade like for like, a favor for a favor, or cohesion that will benefit you both.

# Closing Thoughts: Launch Day

Assuming you didn't open a brick-and-mortar store, the first day you are in business, you should be out roaming the town doing your own marketing. You should be timing your social media accounts to drop interesting posts, videos, and tweets at specific times to drive interest and get you trending in your town. If you're selling a product or an experience, hook up with Groupon and offer a discount to get people interested. Talk to strangers when you're at the bank, grocery store, and gas station. No one should be more excited about your business than you are, and you should do everything you can to convey that excitement to others. If you have a real location or you're working from home, go out and meet your new neighbours. See what their businesses are like, and brainstorm ways you might work together to complement each other's offers.

When you go into business, you must make the most of your time and effort so everything you are doing is working toward growing your business and getting your name out to as many people as possible. You may work harder than you ever have for any other job, but it's totally worth it because the only boss you're working for is yourself. Every sale you make, every customer who goes away satisfied, and every time the phone rings or you get an email, all of that business is because of you. This is your time to be the boss, make the big decisions, and realize your entrepreneurial, financial, and business dreams! Good luck!

# Notes

# MINDING MY BUSINESS

## MINDING MY BUSINESS

# MINDING MY BUSINESS

## MINDING MY BUSINESS

## MINDING MY BUSINESS

# MINDING MY BUSINESS

# MINDING MY BUSINESS

# MINDING MY BUSINESS

## MINDING MY BUSINESS

… MINDING MY BUSINESS

## MINDING MY BUSINESS

# MINDING MY BUSINESS

# MINDING MY BUSINESS

# MINDING MY BUSINESS

MINDING MY BUSINESS

# MINDING MY BUSINESS

# MINDING MY BUSINESS

# MINDING MY BUSINESS

# MINDING MY BUSINESS

## MINDING MY BUSINESS

## MINDING MY BUSINESS

# MINDING MY BUSINESS

# MINDING MY BUSINESS

www.ingramcontent.com/pod-product-compliance
Lightning Source LLC
Chambersburg PA
CBHW031637160426
43196CB00006B/449